# Gentle Redirection of Aggressive and Destructive behavior

A support manual to accompany in-person training

Bobby Newman, Ph.D., BCBA-D

**Published by Dove and Orca**

**ISBN-13:**

**978-1494243043**

**ISBN-10:**

**1494243040**

## Units

# Overview

## Why This Training?

The Gentle Redirection of Aggressive and Destructive behavior (GRAD) program was created in order to satisfy an important need in the developmental disabilities field. Staff members working in facilities serving people with developmental disabilities are trained in crisis management and prevention. Similar trainings are routinely provided to many individuals working in school settings. Training for families and home-based caregivers of individuals with developmental disabilities is not widely available, however.

That this should be the case flies in the face of widely accepted clinical practice conventions and logic. It is a basic statement of fact that families and home-based caregivers spend the majority of time with the individual with developmental disabilities. With this fact in mind, family and home-based caregiver training is recognized as crucial for maintaining behavioral, social, and linguistic gains. Family and home-based caregiver training in general behavioral and educational topics is thus provided as a matter of course, and no one questions the need for such training. Training stops being widely available, however, at the point of crisis management training, with regrettable results. To be blunt, the ability of families and home-based caregivers to prevent and manage physical crises often means the difference between an individual with a developmental disability being able to continue living in a home setting and having to move into a more restrictive environment such as a group home or residence.

The lack of crisis prevention and management programs for families and home-based caregivers has two possible causes:

1. A belief that it is not needed, that training in general behavior management and educational principles is sufficient.
2. A fear of misuse of procedures and consequent injuries to family members or to the individual with the developmental disability.

The first objection can be easily dismissed. If that training in general behavioral and educational concepts truly was sufficient, why would additional crisis intervention and prevention training be needed for staff members in schools and other facilities? Obviously, if staff members working in such facilities require additional training to prevent and to manage crises, then families and caregivers require the same training. I'm not going to lie about it. I have been physically hurt, including dislocations and a hearing loss, in having to perform crisis intervention over the past two plus decades. If that has happened to me after receiving training, do we imagine that things are perfectly safe for those who are not given training?

The second objection is a bit more difficult to answer. It is true that the schools and other facilities serving individuals with developmental disabilities often provide a greater level of supervision and structure, not to mention sheer numbers of persons available, than a typical home setting. For that reason, it is considered safer to provide training in crisis prevention and management in the facilities, as the greater amount of structure and supervision and person-power would help to prevent abuses and accidents.

Even allowing for the possible truth of this argument, however, one has to ask, "then what?" We are still left with the basic truth mentioned above. It is the family and home-based caregivers who are going to spend the majority of time with the individual with the developmental disability. If we accept that there may be physical crises, then what are the families and home-based caregivers supposed to do? Without training, they are left to:

1. "Do the best they can" (which may lead to injuries to family members or to the individual in crisis, or to potentially dangerous object-destructive behavior)
2. Call the police (which may lead to unneeded hospitalizations or legal issues and has

resulted in at least one death within the last few years)

3. Walk on eggshells around the individual for fear of creating a crisis situation (which may lead to long-term behavioral regression as aggressive and destructive behavior is reinforced, or the individual is simply never pushed to improve skills for fear of creating a crisis).

Clearly, each of these options has unacceptable pitfalls associated with it. Training to more efficiently handle crises is therefore crucial for everyone who works and spends time with people with disabilities, families and home-based caregivers included. It is our hope that this training can provide some of the needed information in order to keep everyone safe, learning, and living together happily.

This manual is meant to accompany the live training in GRAD. All participants who wish to complete the training must participate throughout the entire session and pass the written and practical tests that will be provided at the end of the training. Physical intervention techniques will not be pictured nor described in this manual, as we do not want people simply picking up stray copies of this manual and attempting technique without having been coached through their proper use. We apologize for this

**inconvenience, but will be happy to provide follow up video conferencing to fine-tune or relearn technique if anyone finds themselves not remembering how to carry out a particular technique at any point after training is completed.**

**Basic Rules for GRAD**

1. No pain is to be inflicted
2. Not to be used as a punishment procedure
3. No body part is moved beyond its ordinary range of motion
4. Impacts are not used
5. No anger is displayed or felt
6. Voices are not raised
7. Do not intervene unless imminent danger to yourself, individual in crisis, or others
8. If you implement a technique, you are responsible for the safety of the person you are intervening with
9. Be prepared every day
10. Physical interventions are a last resort
11. Be decisive
12. Implement all techniques with safety in mind. Do not obstruct airways at any time, nor cut off circulation. Release and reapply techniques to ensure safety, if crisis is prolonged.

## Long Versus Short-Term Thinking

"We don't get bullied by people under four feet tall." That's a quote from my good friend and fellow clinician Nicole Rogerson of the Lizard Centre in Sydney, Australia. Her sentiment, which is often taken somewhat humorously, nonetheless has an important implication: the person isn't going to stand less than four feet tall forever. Some of you reading this may be thinking about addressing behaviors displayed by individuals who are currently over six feet tall and weigh over 200 pounds.

It is a sad but true fact that while the students get larger and stronger, we who have been in the field for a good while get older and possibly slower, and possibly weaker. Later, I will make a point that we are obligated to train our bodies to mitigate this, but the march of time can only be mitigated just so much.

The point is DO IT NOW. Don't allow inappropriate and aggressive behavior because the individual is currently too small to really hurt you if (s)he hits or kicks. Sooner or later, that won't be the case any longer and the window of time during which behavior management procedures could more easily be conducted will be closed (see *Move with a Purpose*, Newman and Reinecke, 2012).

There is another aspect to long versus short-term thinking that I want to emphasize. That is the issue of moment-to-moment behavior management. A student is having a tantrum because he wants a particular item. The two choices:

1. Give him the item and he will calm down
2. Do not give him the item and the tantrum may possibly escalate.

Think of the implications of these two courses of action. In the first scenario, peace is restored. What has the individual learned, however (see section on reinforcement)? He has learned that if he wants a particular item, and if he tantrums long enough and hard enough, he will get it. This is most likely not the lesson we ever wish to teach. We are therefore left with choice #2, not giving the individual the item (and please beware of the "act out/calm down unit: DO NOT give him the item because he has calmed down. That just teaches a unit of act out so you can receive a reinforcer for calming down).

Choice #2 will likely result in a better long-term outcome, in which the individual is less likely to tantrum in the future. Please understand that acting in accordance with choice #2 will likely lead to temporary, short-term escalations in aggressive behavior, however. Therefore, we must make sure it is safe to undertake this step before doing so (see sections on extinction and extinction bursts). The key here is to ensure safety in the first place, and to teach more appropriate ways to get needs met. There are skills such as "accepting no" and functional equivalence programs (see below) that should be taught in order to avoid ever winding up in such a situation in the first place. The individual with the developmental disability is likely engaging in such behavior because a more socially appropriate one has never been taught or learned. We will go farthest in preventing the need for crisis intervention if we can teach a more socially appropriate way for the individual to get wants and needs met in the future (see section on functional equivalence, for example).

As a final note on this matter, think long and short-term even when thinking about the daily recreational activities of the individual with the developmental disability. While television and the internet can be wonderful educational and entertainment tools, they can also be extremely hazardous. It is no exaggeration to say that in each program where I currently work, there is at least one student who compulsively and nearly continuously repeats lines from television or internet video. It is most often the case that someone is allowing the student to watch, and often to endlessly watch→ rewind→ watch→ rewind→ watch the same 30 seconds of the clip or show for hours at a time. Everyone then has the nerve to be surprised when the student cannot stop verbally repeating the lines and sound effects from the footage when in the school program, or when attempting to get the student to converse with someone else in a community setting. I would personally call this a set up. The person has been set up by being allowed, or sometimes even encouraged, to engage in the repetitive behavior and then is expected to refrain from the behavior that must invariably result.

A short-term benefit - the student was occupied for a time and thus did not require careful supervision - has led to a behavior problem that can be very difficult to solve. When you eventually want to stop the student from perseveratively watching the footage, you may realize you have created another tantrum stimulus. Again, think long-term. Is this something that you want to keep seeing, and is it constructive in the long run, or will it lead to behavioral regression and possible physical crises in the long-term?

## Crisis Management vs. Behavior Treatment Plans

A key distinction that we must keep in mind is between crisis management and behavior treatment plans. Are you having to perform crisis management interventions very frequently? If you are, then you are not really doing crisis management, you are doing behavior treatment interventions (and probably not as efficiently as possible, because if it was going well, you would not be having frequent crisis-level flare-ups).

Briefly stated, crises should be fairly infrequent. If such behavior is occurring frequently, then we are out of the realm of crisis management and are really into the realm of behavior management and behavior treatment plans (see behavior management sections below, and see also www.bacb.com for a listing of individuals who might be able to help in the creation of behavior treatment plans and teaching the more socially appropriate alternate behavior alluded to above. That will likely make the need for frequent crisis intervention greatly lessened).

Professionals are ethically required to create behavior management plans if a client frequently requires crisis intervention. As soon as a crisis occurs, we try to plan for ways to reduce the possibility that this kind of situation will ever occur again. This doesn't mean giving in to the individual or removing all demands, but rather teaching him/her to cope with situations that (s)he might not like. The environment can be arranged to support appropriate responses and to discourage crisis behavior, and parents and caregivers can and should, with support, implement these techniques to a high degree of fidelity and with great success.

## Least Restrictive Treatment

The Least Restrictive Treatment model refers to some related concepts:

1. Services should be provided in the most normalized environment possible, the closest to which a non-developmentally disabled peer would be exposed.
2. All treatments should be reinforcement-based. Punishment procedures are never to be attempted until one has demonstrated with a mountain of data and interventions that non-aversive and reinforcement-based procedures have proven ineffective.

What this amounts to is that we are morally and ethically obligated to never initiate punishment procedures, or any other physically-based crisis management for that matter, unless we have proven that all less intrusive techniques have been ineffective. As we will emphasize repeatedly, crisis management procedures are meant to be a last resort, not a first step.

Understand also that we are not on a level playing field. The individual with the developmental disability who is engaging in the act of aggression is not bound by any set of ethical, moral or legal principles. They are engaging in this behavior because they currently do not have more socially appropriate alternatives in their behavioral repertoire. You do, and you are morally and ethically and legally obligated to handle the aggression in the most gentle way possible. End of story.

## Safety

When we discuss safety, we are talking about a few key concepts. All have the same basic goal of keeping the individual who is displaying the aggression or self-injurious behavior, as well as all other individuals in the environment, safe from harm. For current purposes, though, we are going to make this a bit more specific to remind ourselves of some of our basic safety rules:

1. All techniques must be carried out with the safety of the developmentally disabled individual firmly in mind. This means no moving a body part beyond its ordinary range of motion, never interfering in any way with breathing/airflow or circulation, avoiding inflicting pain, and avoiding impact to the greatest extent possible.
2. As we will discuss at greater length in future chapters on preparedness, safety should be maintained by considering factors such as hazards in the environment (e.g., traffic, glass furniture) and clothing (e.g., high heels, sharp rings) before any difficulties ever arise.

3. Realize that if you have made the determination that a physical intervention is necessary, you have assumed responsibility for the other individual's physical safety.

4. Ethically, as well as practically, physical intervention should be a last resort and all non-physical means of calming should be attempted prior to physically intervening.

As we will discuss in future chapters, preparedness is key. When a crisis occurs, it may be very difficult to address difficulties such as tripping hazards in the environment or inappropriate footwear. The time to analyze such easily correctable dangers is well before there is ever any sign of crisis.

The other key that we must emphasize right now is the physical safety of the individual who is engaging in the behavior that is causing the crisis in terms of the application of physical technique. There will be times when you must use variations from the techniques that you will be taught. This can happen due to the varying sizes of the individual who is demonstrating the dangerous behavior and the person attempting to provide support, for example. The demonstrated technique may not be safe to use if you as the person providing support do not have the physical strength to

**ensure the other individual's safety when executing a particular technique, for example. All techniques, however, must be carried out with the basic rules above kept in mind. Pain must never be used, nor a body part moved beyond ordinary range of motion, nor impact used, nor must airways or circulation ever be compromised. Again, the time to think of, design and practice, technique would be well before there ever is a crisis.**

**"In the moment" is a difficult time to design technique that ensures safety to all.**

# Behavioral Concepts

## Reinforcement

A reinforcer is a consequence that follows a given behavior, and makes that behavior more likely to be displayed in the future. This definition is simple enough, and serves our current purposes. We will make finer distinctions, but before we do, it will be important to make sure we understand the implications of this central concept.

As I put it in my book *Behavioral Detectives*, reinforcement is all about what happens, not about what you intended to do. Very often in clinical practice, one comes across individuals who are delivering consequences that they think are reinforcers, but they are not in fact delivering reinforcers. Conversely, one often finds individuals delivering consequences that they think are not reinforcers, yet they are. The clinical literature is full of reports where a given programmed consequence was accidentally reinforcing the behavior in question (e.g., using time-out when someone did not want to be in the situation in the first place, as described in that same *Behavioral Detectives* book).

The key point is that reinforcers are as individual as people are. In the famous *Harry* training film, for example, it was experimentally demonstrated that being placed in physical restraints was reinforcing the self-injurious behavior of the individual. I'm fairly certain that the clinicians who had been working with Harry prior to the film did not set out to deliberately reinforce his self-injury, but they did so nonetheless. This is, in fact, a common consideration in crisis intervention. Are we possibly accidentally reinforcing the behavior though our crisis intervention techniques?

Another point to consider is that all consequences are not reinforcers. You may deliver a consequence following a given behavior, but if that consequence does not make the given behavior more likely in the future, then you have not delivered a reinforcer. As we will discuss below, data collection is very important, ensuring that you keep track of what you are doing and what effect it has on behavior.

Making another distinction, reinforcers can be divided into positive and negative. BOTH MAKE THE BEHAVIOR THEY FOLLOW MORE LIKELY. NEGATIVE REINFORCEMENT AND PUNISHMENT ARE TWO DIFFERENT THINGS! Forgive the textual shouting, but this confusion is common and can truly damage behavioral programming.

An easy way to remember this is that the techniques are defined by what happens to the behavior (becoming more likely in the future if you have delivered a reinforcer) and what you have done in terms of the delivery of consequence. Think of it mathematically: any time you ADD something to the situation, that is a POSITIVE procedure. Any time you TAKE SOMETHING

**AWAY from the situation, that is a NEGATIVE procedure. Some examples:**

1. **You ask a student to deliver a message. You give a "high five" and praise after he delivers the message, and his tendency to follow requests to deliver messages in the future increases. This is a positive reinforcement scenario (you have *added* praise and a "high five" and that served to increase the probability of the behavior).**
2. **You ask a student to deliver a message. The student begins to cry and bang his head. You withdraw the request and your physical presence, not wanting to upset the individual. You notice that the future probability of crying and head-banging increase when you make requests. This is a negative reinforcement scenario (you have *taken away* your request and presence, and that served to increase the future probability of the tantrum behavior).**

**An additional point to remember is that just because you have established something as a reinforcer does not mean that it will remain one. People "satiate" on particular reinforcers, meaning the reinforcer can lose its potency if it is used too often. In the course of our training we will discuss:**

a. primary reinforcers (those you do not need to learn to find reinforcing)

b. secondary or conditioned reinforcers (those you needed to learn to find reinforcing)

c. generalized reinforcers (those that can be traded in for other reinforcers)

d. Premack/activity reinforcers (a high probability behavior being used to reinforce a lower probability behavior).

There are implications to each of these different types of reinforcers that we will discuss (see definitions in *Behaviorspeak* and *Behaviorask*).

## FBAs and Determinism

It is a basic assumption of behavioral science that behavior follows particular laws. We call this "behavioral determinism." It simply means that behavior follows particular rules, and if we can determine the variables controlling behavior, we can understand the behavior. If we can change those variables, we can change the behavior. If determinism were not assumed, putting treatment plans in place would make absolutely no sense. What would be the point of a behavior treatment plan if behavior were truly just random, or if it was based entirely on biological or internal influences?

To determine what is causing behavior, we conduct something called a Functional Behavioral Assessment, or a Functional Behavioral Analysis (depending on whether we do naturalistic observation or actually manipulate particular variables). The steps to these are outlined in *Behaviorspeak* and *Behaviorask*. As mentioned in a few places within our manual, there are professionals, Board Certified Behavior Analysts, whose specialty is doing precisely this, and such professionals can be contacted through www.BACB.com.

As an example of this and its implications for the person's functioning, consider the example from the prior chapter. A functional analysis has been conducted and it has been determined that a student has learned to tantrum and to engage in self-injury when requests are made because this leads to people withdrawing requests. We would call this "avoidance behavior" or possibly "escape behavior" (depending on whether the person is attempting to avoid something which has not yet begun, or is attempting to get away from an activity that is on-going).

Now that we know the function of the behavior, we can do something about it. Our behavior treatment plan would likely emphasize two concurrent activities:

1. not allowing the student to use this behavior to avoid (to anticipate future vocabulary, we will put the avoidance behavior on extinction by no longer reinforcing it)
2. teaching the student a more socially appropriate way to avoid or postpone unwanted activities

Until we know the function of a given behavior, however, it is difficult to create treatment plans. What if the behavior were actually attention-seeking (i.e., we did the functional analysis incorrectly)? We would be teaching the student irrelevant skills, and our treatment plan would likely reinforce the behavior we were seeking to eliminate and thereby make the behavioral problem much worse.

## Extinction and Extinction Bursts

Extinction simply refers to not reinforcing a behavior when it occurs. It is said that a behavior is "put on extinction" when we decide that we are no longer going to reinforce a given behavior. Note that when we are talking about extinction, or indeed any particular behavior treatment plan, we talk about applying the procedure to the behavior and not to the individual. In other words, it would be correct to say we are placing John's tantrum on extinction. It would not be correct to say we are placing John on extinction. Similarly, we reinforce John's requesting, we do not reinforce John. While such distinctions may seem like mere semantics, it is important in that:

1. we are using terminology correctly
2. it helps us to remember exactly what behavior is targeted

Please note a common confusion and avoid it: extinction is not the same thing as ignoring someone. Extinction means eliminating the reinforcer that has been provided following a particular behavior. I can eliminate a reinforcing reaction to a student's spitting, for example, without ever ceasing to pay attention to a student. Extinction means eliminating the reinforcer, and we first need to determine what the reinforcer is.

Once one has determined what is reinforcing a given behavior, one can implement an extinction plan. When considering doing this, however, one must be keenly aware of something called an extinction burst. Briefly and colloquially stated, the concept behind the extinction burst is that before a behavior gets better, it is going to temporarily get worse.

When an extinction procedure is implemented and an extinction burst occurs, behavior generally bursts in one or all of three very important ways:

1. behavior bursts in frequency (it is done more often)
2. behavior bursts in magnitude (it is done with a greater degree of intensity)
3. behavior bursts in variability (it is done in different ways)

It is crucial to appreciate the extinction burst, as one who is not familiar with it might mistakenly believe that a plan was making a behavior worse, when in fact it is only a temporary extinction burst.

Second and perhaps even more crucially, the extinction burst must be considered when deciding whether or not an extinction procedure can be implemented in the first place. What if the person's behavior is capable of bursting to the point where the plan can no longer be safely done? In our opening, I mentioned a hearing loss. I was hit by a student who was well over 300 pounds and could run the 100 yard dash in under ten seconds. I never wrote an extinction plan for him in my life. While he engaged in tantrums very infrequently, when they did occur they were very dangerous due to his size and strength. I therefore never wrote extinction plans for his behavior, and relied on other plans instead. A similar story can be told regarding a student who engaged in very simple running away that had a very straightforward "chase me game" function. While it was a very simple behavior to understand and extinction would likely have been the treatment plan of choice, the physical layout was too dangerous to allow running without her being chased.

Please keep this firmly in mind when considering treatment plans. Very often, the most dangerous behavior problems have been created by well-meaning individuals who attempted extinction plans, but then had to abandon them when the burst occurred and the clinicians discovered too late that they were forced to terminate the plan during the burst and thereby reinforce the new, much more dangerous, behavior (consider a student who was previously striking his face with an open palm, who during the extinction burst begins to strike his face with a closed fist and then bang his head into the table). Consider also our next section on possibly intermittently reinforcing this new, much more dangerous variation on the behavior. Put yourself in the place of the student. If behavior has been

**maintained by intermittent reinforcement, the student does not know how long or how intensely they need to tantrum, but they do know it will achieve their desired end at some point.**

## Continuous Vs. Intermittent Reinforcement

Reinforcers must be delivered according to some system. A very basic distinction is between continuous reinforcement and intermittent reinforcement. Continuous reinforcement simply means that every time a particular behavior is displayed, a reinforcer is delivered. Intermittent simply means that less than every time a behavior is displayed, a reinforcer is delivered. With intermittent reinforcement, the delivery system may be specific (e.g., every third response) or it may follow some random sequence (e.g., *roughly* every third response, but sometimes one, sometimes five, sometimes three, etc.).

The delivery system has important implications for behavior treatment plans. Consider the distinction. A soda machine works on continuous reinforcement. Every time you put in the money, the soda comes out. People learn to use the machine quickly, and behavior maintains nicely. When the machine breaks down, however, people generally begin banging on the machine (demonstrating an extinction burst) and the money-inserting behavior ceases quickly. We call this having very little resistance to extinction.

Consider, in contrast, a slot machine. It only pays off every once in a while. You don't expect the slot machine to deliver a reinforcer every time. Note that this more intermittent reinforcement does not generally lead to people beating up slot machines as with a broken soda machine, and people do not stop putting money in. Very often, they put all the money they have into the machine. We consider this behavior as having a great deal of resistance to extinction.

Translate this discussion into our behavioral considerations. Suppose a student has been screaming to get desired items. If the behavior has been previously being reinforced on a continuous reinforcement basis, it will likely disappear shortly after the extinction procedure is implemented (like a broken soda machine). If the behavior has been maintained by intermittent reinforcement, however, the behavior will likely have much more resistance to extinction and last for a great deal longer (like people in front of a slot machine). You will also likely be reinforcing a much worse variation on the behavior (see previous section on extinction bursts).

As a final thought on this, please note that procedures are not good or bad in and of themselves. We have been talking about extinction bursts as dangerous, but extinction bursts are also used to fine tune behavior by withholding reinforcement for cruder attempts at a behavior (as when we shape language or athletic performance). Intermittent reinforcement, we have said, leads to behavior that has more resistance to extinction (is longer lasting in the absence of reinforcement). Don't you want that kind of frustration

**tolerance for tasks that may be difficult for a student, such as learning to tie shoes?**

## Behavior Goals and Behavior Treatment Plans

It is important to have very clearly defined behavioral goals. Think about the failure of vague behavior goals such as "I'm going to try to get to the gym more." Forgive me, but I could watch you for nine years and not know if you're trying to get to the gym more. But what if the goal were written in the form of,

"Mike will ride the exercise bike, for 20 minutes at 70% of aerobic capacity, on Monday and Wednesday and Friday night at the New York Sports Club"?

Now a little careful observation will ensure that there is no confusion as to whether or not the behavior goal is being met. Therefore, it is always a good idea to specify behavior goals with the following characteristics:

1. What should the person do?
2. How much of it should they do?
3. Under what circumstances should they do it?

Having clear behavior goals and behavioral definitions is crucial. If we do not have clear definitions, for example, we may have inconsistency among staff. If we do not have a clear definition, I may perform the treatment plan when you don't, or note on the data sheets that the behavior has been performed when you do not, etc. Training observers to a solid level of what we call inter-observer agreement is also often required.

Behavior treatment plans should also be written in such a form that there is no confusion regarding when plans are supposed to be implemented and when they are not. I recommend having the following elements in a treatment plan to eliminate any confusion or ambiguities:

1. A clearly stated behavioral goal of what the student should do (not what he should *not* do).
2. The technical name of the behavior change procedure(s) in place
3. A practical description of the behavior treatment plan, saying when the plan should and should not be implemented
4. The rationale for the use of the plan (i.e., a statement of the function of the behavior and how the plan addresses function)
5. Considerations, including anything special one needs to know in order to implement the plan, as well as any concerns regarding potential problems with the plan

6. The data collection system to monitor plan effectiveness
7. Mastery criterion (when are we done with the plan?)

Having clearly written behavioral definitions, goals and treatment plans will go a long way towards eliminating confusion or accidental intermittent reinforcement of behavior problems.

## Triggers and Stimulus Control

We have previously discussed control of behavior by consequences (e.g., positive and negative reinforcers). Behavior can also be controlled by stimuli that occur prior to the behavior occurring. Such behaviors are said to be under "stimulus control." Consider the simple example of a traffic light. A green light signals that going through the light should be safe. A red light signals that there might be danger from cars coming perpendicular to yourself, as well as the possibility of a ticket from a monitoring police officer.

Often behavior falls under such stimulus control, as when, for example, a student's behavior is very different in the presence of one individual than it is in the presence of another individual. This may indicate that one individual is much more consistent and effective in carrying out treatment plans than the other. The key here, obviously, is to arrange things so that everyone is equally efficient in carrying out treatment plans, and then any such differences depending on who the individual is with should disappear.

Another concept in control by stimuli antecedent to the behavior is that of a behavioral trigger. This is where knowledge of the person you are working with can be crucial. Triggers for individuals are highly individualized. One student, for example, might be likely to have a behavioral outburst in a crowd, when (s)he feels constricted and/or there is unwanted physical contact. Another individual may be more likely to have difficulties in very loud situations, noise being the trigger. Another individual may have difficulties in the presence of a particular individual who engages in behavior that (s)he finds troubling.

When there are identifiable triggers for behavior, one has two main options:

1. One can avoid these situations
2. One can, under control and with a plan, gradually expose the individual to the trigger stimuli as a means of helping him/her learn to respond appropriately to the trigger (e.g., learning to say “It’s too loud, I want to step outside” instead of hitting someone in response to noise).

## Data Keeping Plans

It is basic to good behavior management planning that we keep accurate data to assess how the target behavior is responding to intervention. Without careful data, we are left with guessing whether or not a behavior is responding to intervention, and such guesses can often be inaccurate (as when the frequency of a truly annoying or dangerous behavior is over-estimated because it is so annoying or dangerous). Inaccurate or absent data can lead to keeping treatment plans in place that are not truly being effective, or terminating plans that actually are effective (but may only be having slow and gradual effects).

What follows are just a few of the most basic and common types of data collection strategies. There are many. The key is to pick the one that best captures the dimension of the behavior we are seeking to measure to assess the effectiveness of our treatment plan.

1. Frequency: How many times did the behavior occur?
2. Rate: How many times did the behavior occur per some unit of time?
3. Latency: How long did it take for the behavior to get started once some trigger was provided?
4. Duration: How long did the behavior last?

5. **Magnitude**: Some measure of intensity of behavior, often done on a scale.
6. **% Correct**: How many times, out of a given number of opportunities, did the person engage in the behavior?
7. **Initial Probe**: Did the person engage in the behavior at the first opportunity?

The mode of data collection is important to consider when one first begins to draft a treatment plan. The data collection plan must be realistic, given resources. If it seems that the plan is not working, one factor one must consider prior to terminating the plan is whether the data that are being collected effectively monitor the behavior in question.

## Generalization and Maintenance

It is one thing to get a behavior under control. Working consistently with students in a school program, for example, you may be able to get a particular behavior eliminated comparatively easily. Will the behavior change go across settings (generalization), however, and will the benefits continue after you have terminated the treatment plan (maintenance)?

It is a truism of behavior intervention that one must plan for generalization and maintenance; one cannot simply assume that they will occur. Most often, in fact, generalization and maintenance will not occur unless you have specifically set things up to ensure that it will occur.

In order to facilitate generalization, one varies all non-essential aspects of the teaching situation. One teaches, for example, across a wide variety of settings (particularly the key settings where one wants to see the behavior, such as in the home or community). One varies instructors, after assuring that they are all conversant in the particulars of the treatment plans. One varies time of day, phrasings of instructions, etc., in the attempt to capture conditions as they will exist in other settings and make sure that the individual can still respond as they did in the original training location.

Maintenance is similar in that you are creating conditions to encourage the behavior to occur beyond the original training conditions. In this case, however, what you are planning for is how to encourage the behavior to keep occurring after the termination of the formal behavior treatment plan. In order to accomplish this, some of the most common strategies are:

1. Training others in the setting to carry through on the treatment plan just as you have been
2. If the individual is changing locations, teaching others in the new setting to carry through on the treatment plan just as you have been
3. Teaching self-management skills to the individual (self-monitoring and self-reinforcement)
4. Fading reinforcement and prompting strategies so that control of the behavior is transferred to naturally-occurring stimuli

Planning for generalization and maintenance must be part of all behavior treatment efforts. If a behavior only changes in your presence, or while you are actively involved, you are basically agreeing to stay on in a 24 hour a day capacity, and that is hardly conducive to increasing independent functioning.

## "Catch 'em Being Good"

The idea behind "catch 'em being good" is very simple: reinforce when you see behavior you want to see, and then you won't have to be responding to behavior you don't want to see. By definition, if you reinforce a behavior, you'll see it more often. That leaves less and less time for inappropriate behavior to occur.

This is not only sound behavior management, but it avoids some common behavioral traps. One such trap is the idea that "he *should* show the behavior I want because he just *should*." Thinking about it realistically, however, we all engage in behavior we shouldn't, and don't engage enough in behavior that we should. Simply leaving it to *should* is not likely to lead to success. We need to stack the deck in order to succeed.

Catching the person being good also makes it very clear what behavior you are looking for. Feel free to use descriptive praise: "hey, I really like the way you...." By doing this, you'll eliminate ambiguity in terms of desired behavior.

Catching a person being good also resets the behavioral relationship. Too often, behavior is not noticed unless it is inappropriate. This is what we grow up with. How often does a schoolteacher reprimand a student who is calling out versus congratulating a student who is doing the right thing? How often does a police officer comment on safe driving versus pulling someone over for speeding? Our society basically seems set up only for catching people doing the wrong thing, not the right thing. Within the micro-societies of our families and small facilities, however, we have the opportunity to change that, to put everything on a much more pleasant and positive footing.

That being said, and as alluded to elsewhere in the manual, please be careful of the "act out/calm down" unit. When someone has just had a behavioral outburst is not necessarily the time to be engaging in extreme levels of reinforcement. There is nothing wrong with acknowledging "I like the way you've calmed down and are now talking about what is bothering you." There is something, wrong, however, with offering candy to get someone up off the ground, or after they have just stood up after a struggle to get them up. Individuals can easily learn to engage in inappropriate behavior in order to earn a reinforcer for stopping that behavior. The best way to avoid this, of course, is to remember to catch them being good. Reinforce appropriate behavior that you want to keep seeing, *before* any problem behavior occurs, and there will be less likelihood of the person ever engaging in the inappropriate behavior in the first place.

## De-escalation Tools

When we discuss de-escalation tools, we are talking about techniques implemented before physical intervention to help the person to calm him/herself and manage behavior. As we have repeated throughout this manual, these techniques should be tried before any physical intervention is used (physical intervention always being last resort).

The key to de-escalation is to know the person well in terms of how (s)he responds to particular strategies. Talking a great deal to one person may make him/her feel that you are attempting to help and this will be calming. Talking a great deal to another individual will be very annoying and overwhelming and may increase agitation markedly. Knowing the person you are with is crucial; joking about a situation as suggested below may help some people to feel better, but might make others feel you are not taking their concerns seriously.

What follows are some very common de-escalation strategies. In keeping with the above discussion, some of these techniques may be appropriate for the individual you are considering, while some will be counter-productive. We provide these ten only as a jumping off point for various strategies that can be attempted.

1. **Removing the individual**: If the trigger can be identified and as the person indicates discomfort, help them to make their agitation known appropriately and leave the setting.
2. **Reassure**: Verbally indicate to the person that you know something is bothering them and you are attempting to figure out what it is and help them to address it.
3. **Physical contact**: Touch the individual on hand, arm or shoulder to indicate that you are there with them and supportive and know there is a building difficulty.
4. **Humor**: Joke about the situation to try to defuse.
5. **Ask questions**: Try to get the individual to verbalize what it is that is bothering them.
6. **Use visual cues**: Some people, particularly when agitated, do not process spoken language well. Using written or picture cues such as "first/then" may be helpful. This will often require prior preparation in terms of pictures/icons, of course, although writing can be done at nearly any time.

7. **Remind of consequences**: Remind the individual of what they are earning (e.g., "don't forget that we are working towards having a snack soon"), or what the possible ramifications of having a physical crisis are (e.g., if out in public and someone might call the police, etc.).

8. **Distraction/Redirection**: If the trigger is having to wait, or having to endure some sort of troubling situation, attempts to distract/redirect through conversation or engaging in other tasks/conversation can be attempted.

9. **Eliminate the problem**: As long as you are not working on a desensitization program, if you know that a particular stimulus is troubling to the individual, can it be eliminated? For example, is a television or radio too loud? Can we head to a less crowded area?

10. **Coach**: Provide suggestions to the individual for how they might be able to help themselves, or attempt to encourage them that they can work through the difficulty (perhaps combine with #2, reassuring them that they can get through this and you are with them?).

**We repeat, however, that there is no substitute for knowing the person you are working with. There will likely be other strategies not mentioned here that will be equally or more effective. We present these only to provide an indication of possibilities for de-escalation techniques.**

## Functional Equivalence

One de-escalation strategy that bears special mention is the idea of functional equivalence. The idea behind "functional equivalence" is that one can reduce/replace a maladaptive behavior by teaching a more socially appropriate one that will take its place. As an example, consider a student who has learned to bang his head as an attention-seeking response. We can put this behavior on extinction by not allowing the head-banging to get him attention. More important, however, we must teach the student a more socially appropriate way to seek attention (for example, by raising his hand).

There is an extensive literature describing this sub-area of behavior management and teaching (see work by Carr and Durand, for example), showing how teaching relatively simple responses such as holding up cards with messages on them can eliminate the need for the student to engage in the behavior he had previously displayed. It is important to note that the student need not even be able to read what is on the card, just to learn that holding up that piece of paper gets people to leave you alone for five minutes, or get you more time on the computer, or get you a new set of materials when you get bored, etc.

It is important that the alternate response you are trying to teach be relatively easy to perform (it has to be less trouble to perform than the behavior that is being replaced) and everyone has to honor the response. This will mean making sure everyone in contact with the student knows the treatment plan and understands the alternate response. It has happened, for example, that an American Sign Language communication was taught, but this proved not to be functional because people in contact with the student did not understand the communication.

# Practicalities

## Keeping Calm and it is Not Personal

It is often difficult to remember that an individual who is punching, kicking, or throwing objects at you is not doing so because of some personal vendetta. This is exacerbated when there is real physical danger involved, when the person demonstrating the behavior is large and strong and capable of causing serious physical injury, and the person may be making personal remarks against you. So how could it be that the person in question is making personal insults (using your name, discussing your weight or hair loss or other such personal issues) and yet the situation should not be considered personal?

What must be remembered is that the person engaging in the behavior in question generally does not have other, more socially appropriate, coping skills in his or her behavioral repertoire. What you are seeing is the result of a skill *deficit*. The person may not have the language to make their wants/needs known, or the skills to deal with a particular stressor at this particular time. Even if the individual is able to handle the stressor under other circumstances, the individual may be so overwhelmed by current conditions that the person is resorting to the behavior you are seeing in order to get current wants/needs known and addressed. That this is the case can be inferred from the functional equivalence literature discussed elsewhere in this manual.

Keeping calm is most important in crisis situations. When individuals panic, and this is often what causes behavioral crises in the first place, something called the fight or flight reflex is triggered. When a person enters “fight or flight mode,” adrenaline flows through the body. Breathing gets quick and shallow, hearts pound, muscles tense. This is the body preparing to fight off a threat or run away from it, a throwback to earlier days in human history when threats tended to be physical instead of social. It is not consistent with the calm and careful execution of technique that is required to maintain everyone’s safety in a crisis, or to deliver an oral report in your college class.

As will be discussed next, practice is a key. The first time you need to remember how to get someone’s hands out of your hair should not be when there is an actual crisis and someone is pulling your hair. The first time you have to remember how to execute a technique, and actually execute it, should be in controlled practice, at half speed, with someone whom you trust. I would add that a great many practice sessions would be useful before you ever face a real crisis. You need to develop new reflexes, where calm execution will replace the panicked responses that might lead to injury to self or other. A panicked lashing out reaction, where you actually aggress back at the individual may occur, or

**you may simply physically freeze. Neither response is constructive in the crisis situation.**

## Practice, Practice

During trainings not related to crisis intervention training, I make it a point to grab the hair of someone sitting in the front row and quickly ask, “Ok, now what do you do?”

People are often taken a bit aback by my behavior, but I have a real point I’m trying to make. The first time you have to handle a crisis situation should not be an actual crisis. I strongly suggest at least bi-weekly practice in crisis management techniques in order to keep one’s reflexes sharp. When someone has a hold of your hair is most definitely not the time you want to be sitting and thinking, “Oh yeah, what am I supposed to do in this situation?”

Your reflexes must be sharp, and the techniques second nature. This is not just for your own safety, but for the safety of the person who is engaging in the aggression as well. Simply trusting your own reflexes if you haven’t practiced may lead you into a panic move which gets yourself injured, or lashing out against the individual and inadvertently injuring him/her. This is particularly true for larger/stronger crisis intervention responders, or those who have taken some type of self-defense training such as at a martial arts dojo. Such training is rarely done with Least Restrictive Treatment in mind, and trusting the reflexes developed in such training may lead to injury to self or other.

## Dress for It: Be Ready Every Day

Take a look at yourself right now. What, if anything, are you wearing that might be a detriment if a crisis management procedure were suddenly needed? I will list only a few of the most common dangers I see on the part of staff and family members on a daily basis:

1. Dangling earrings
2. Sharp metal wristwatches
3. Sharp rings on fingers
4. Opened toed shoes
5. Shoes with no backs on them
6. High heels
7. Shoes with soles that provide no traction
8. Neck-ties that can instantly become ready-made nooses
9. Hair that cannot be secured on a moment's notice
10. Chokers (if ever there was an appropriately named accessory!)
11. Dangling necklaces
12. Sharp bracelets
13. Rings through various facial piercings
14. Fingernails that resemble a wolverine's or a Tassie Devil's
15. Glasses that cannot be quickly and easily removed
16. Hot coffee in your hand, or in reaching distance

**While we are considering, clothing, etc. please also consider the clothing on the individual you are working with. Are any of the above-mentioned hazards present? If so, that might have to be considered in terms of keeping the individual safe in the future. Please also consider other assorted details. If the individual is given to kicking, for example, dressing the individual in steel-toed construction boots might not the best idea I've ever heard.**

**The key here is to plan ahead and be ready for when any crisis should occur. I have what I jokingly call my "behavior geek" or "action nerd" wristwatch. It is a $12 digital rubber thing, but it has a stop watch function built in and can count up and count down to help me collect data for behavior treatment plans. More importantly, it is never going to hurt anyone. Even if someone had it rubbed against their skin during a crisis intervention procedure, it would cause no injury or pain. I cannot say the same for many of the watches that I see many people wearing on a daily basis. At times, I have even used pocket watches, looking like a throwback to some earlier time. It was what was necessary at that moment. If I could possibly get away with it, indeed if I would not look some kind of bizarre super-hero wannabe, all of my shirts that I would wear every day would be made from the compression-fit line of the**

Under Armour™ company (wicking moisture, being durable, and providing virtually nothing to grab).

Think also, please, when scheduling activities. It is never a good idea to go out alone with an individual who is given to behavioral outbursts if you cannot handle such physical outbursts alone. It would be better to wait and go out only when sufficient people are available to manage any possible outbursts. This need not only be a matter of one individual who is too large for you to manage. Having two individuals with you who may run off would create the same unworkable situation. There's only one of you, and you can't chase people who are running in opposite directions. As we will talk about in a future heading, be realistic.

Finally, always consider physical setting. Do this before there is a crisis situation. What are the hazards in the area? Is there a great deal of glass that can break and become a ubiquitous cutting threat? Perhaps that should be eliminated until aggressive behavior has become very unlikely. Are there heavy objects that can be thrown? Are there very sharp objects present, or sharp edges on furniture? What are tripping hazards? What are escape routes or possible running away risks? Consider this before the crisis hits, and you won't have to think of it in the moment. If you haven't thought about this, think about it as soon as you realize there may be a crisis and act accordingly.

**We repeat the mantra. Think as much as possible out ahead of time, and you'll be less likely to have avoidable injuries occur to self or others.**

## Be Decisive

If you have determined that a crisis is indeed occurring, and someone will be injured if intervention does not occur, then do it. In the 25 plus years that I have been doing this work, I have seen more individuals be injured by someone being too hesitant to intervene, or intervening in a half-hearted way, than by people coming in too heavy-handedly.

This is not to suggest that you become "trigger happy," however, and seek to intervene at the drop of a hat. It is a suggestion that you must learn to realistically appraise situations and intervene when intervention is necessary. Knowing the person you are working with is crucial in terms of learning to understand their behavior patterns and triggers.

If you have made the determination that intervening is necessary, then do so. Use sufficient energy to keep yourself and the other individual safe. Remember our basic rules. Any time that you perform an intervention that involves you physically contacting another individual, you are assuming responsibility for the safety of that individual. That will mean performing any necessary actions with the

**necessary decisiveness to see that the techniques are carried out properly and safely.**

## Be Realistic

If there is a procedure that you know you cannot do safely, do not attempt it. As the Star Wars™ character Yoda put it, “Do, or do not. There is no try.”

“Trying” to do something that is physically impossible for you, if there is any other possible option, is not a smart strategy. Given my own size, it is unlikely that I can single-handedly “wrap” a six foot five inch, 300 pound man. My arms simply would not be long enough. Given a physical crisis situation, I would have to consider all possible options to maintain safety other than my directly physically moving in. For example, can I deflect any aggression long enough to help the individual to calm himself through non-physical means? Is there a safe place I can move any other vulnerable individuals? Are there any throwing/breaking hazards immediately present that I can eliminate?

Will there be times caution must be thrown to the wind and an attempt that is likely to fail be undertaken? It is possible. If out alone with someone whom you cannot manage if a physical crisis arises, and that person begins to run towards oncoming traffic, all bets are off. You must obviously try to stop them any safe way possible. But to repeat our earlier warnings, one should be wary about ever creating such situations in the first place. If you know you are with a person who is given to behavioral outbursts and you know that you cannot handle such crises alone, do not go out alone with this individual in the first place. If you find yourself in such a situation, you may have to act in ways to prevent crises from occurring, even if it is counter to good behavior management (such as providing requested food items, even if you would prefer that the individual not have it). While this is not desirable, it is better than a physical crisis that leads to injury to self or other.

## Get in Shape

Getting real-life here for a moment, I stand about five foot five or six, and weigh about 160 pounds. In other words, I am far from a large or intimidating-looking person, certainly far smaller than the 200-300 pound individuals I sometimes work with.

I do, however, lift weights at the gym 3 days a week, and try to take 5-15 mile runs two to three of the other days during the week. I run marathons a few times a year. I used to try to do seven days a week of structured training, but I have found that my now 46 year old body needs days off for recovery and for optimal functioning.

I'm not going to lie about it. Sometimes this means getting up very early in the morning to take my run before my wife and son wake up, or to make sure I'm on time for an early meeting. It often means stopping at the gym on the way home from work, or paying high day rates at the local gym when I'm working on the road. Given that I am not naturally the largest person in the world, however, I consider it an essential part of my job in order to function efficiently. I must be fast enough to be able to move through a building quickly if needed, and have the physical strength and stamina to execute a technique properly if required to do so.

In other words, physical conditioning is not a luxury. It is not about vanity and looking good in front of a mirror, although if that will help to motivate you, more power to you. The issue is being able to do what needs to be done to keep yourself and others safe. Having well-trained, toned and properly stretched muscles, as well as a healthy cardio-vascular system, is going to cut down on injuries and increase your effectiveness.

## Physical intervention is the Last Resort

We have said this repeatedly throughout the manual and repeat it here for final emphasis. Physically intervening with an individual in crisis should be a last resort, when injury to self or other is imminent.

As repeated throughout the manual, there are practical and ethical reasons for this. To intervene physically is to take the risk of someone getting injured. That is a simple and obvious truth. If one is going to assume this risk, therefore, there must be an even greater risk of injury to self or others if you do *not* intervene, in order to ethically justify the intervention. Some individuals with developmental disabilities, in their panic, may engage in escalated levels of behavior if an intervention is implemented. Obviously, this increases the risk of injury to all. This is a further argument, obviously, against physical intervention if danger to self or others is not immediate.

Ethically speaking, to implement a physical intervention is to invade someone else's body space, and in a sense to temporarily take away their personal autonomy. This may cause feelings of discomfort, and we can only ethically justify this if it is in the name of keeping the individual or someone else physically safe.

## What if it Doesn't Work?

You are learning specific techniques during the course of this training for handling particular types of physical crisis situations. An obvious question is "what is the technique doesn't work?" In other words, you have implemented the technique as designed (e.g., an attempt to terminate a bite or hair pull) and the technique was unsuccessful at terminating the crisis.

Before we go into alternates, we must return to an earlier point. Is it necessary to do an intervention in the first place (i.e., is danger to self or others imminent)? Also, can you perform a technique safely? Remember our earlier discussion of being realistic. If you are not able to carry out techniques safely, it is not wise to attempt a technique halfway. You may be better off attempting to use all techniques that are not based on physical intervention, or otherwise attempting to make the situation safe and helping the individual to de-escalate. There will be times, however, when you have to physically intervene and the intervention you attempt does not work to address the crisis.

This will happen on occasion. Sometimes the solution is to perform the technique again. Sometimes the solution is to attempt a new technique. There are variations on particular techniques, alternative versions of given procedures, that will be demonstrated during

**training. If one technique does not work, then an alternate may be attempted.**

**There will be times, however, when this will not be successful. As described above, sometimes differing body sizes will make particular techniques ineffective or dangerous to implement. In such cases, you may have no choice but to improvise a new technique that suits your body size and the situation. These must always be done, however, in keeping with our basic rules (do not move a body part beyond its range of ordinary motion, no pain, do not obstruct airways or circulation, minimize impact, etc.).**

**It seems like a cop-out to say "improvise," but being realistic, that is the answer that inevitably comes up at the end of such discussions. After one or two instances, however, parameters are generally established that let you know what variations on technique will be effective.**

## Finding Additional Help

We strongly recommend attempting to obtain additional resources, especially at the beginning of your effort. As we have repeated in several places, there is a difference between occasional crisis management and frequent behavior problems that require specific behavior treatment plans. The consumer information page of www.BACB.com (the international Behavior Analyst Certification Board) has a registry of certified individuals, broken down by state and area, with e-mail links to the certified individuals listed there.

Additionally, one can approach local state and non-profit agencies serving people with developmental disabilities (in New York, for example, this is the OPWDD, Office for Persons With Developmental Disabilities, formerly OMRDD, Office of Mental Retardation and Developmental Disabilities). Such state agencies and non-profit organizations can guide you in the finding of resources such as in-home rehabilitation support, respite services, parent training, and other sometimes vital supports.

## Sample Test

### True/False

1. All consequences are reinforcers.
2. Planning ahead can be the best means of preventing crises, or minimizing their impact when they do occur.
3. You should practice techniques repeatedly with people you trust before you ever implement them in a crisis situation.
4. What you wear is irrelevant to crisis intervention.
5. Negative reinforcement is the same thing as punishment.
6. Physical intervention should be a last resort.
7. When you begin an intervention, you assume responsibility for the other person's safety.
8. Parents and caregivers don't need crisis intervention training.
9. Providing impacts like punching and kicking is a part of crisis intervention technique.
10. Conducting a functional behavioral assessment/analysis is something just anyone can do.

### Multiple Choice

11. GRAD techniques rule out the use of:

a. pain
b. moving a limb beyond ordinary range of motion
c. cutting off breathing or circulation
d. impact
e. all of the above

12. A good behavior goal should specify:
    a. what the person should do
    b. how much of it the person should do
    c. under what circumstances the behavior should be done
    d. all of the above
13. When confronted with a crisis situation, one should:
    a. get angry
    b. keep calm
    c. attempt to de-escalate in a non-physical manner
    d. both B and C
14. When considering behavior:
    a. long-term benefits are always paramount
    b. short-term benefits are always paramount
    c. long-term benefits are generally paramount, but we must also consider momentary safety
    d. short-term benefits are generally paramount, and momentary safety does not matter

**15. Intermittent reinforcement:**

a. **generally leads to behavior that goes away quickly**
b. **generally lead to behavior that is long-lasting**
c. **has no real impact on behavior**
d. **means we ignore the person**

## References


Carr, E. G., & Durand, V. M. (1985). Reducing behavior problems through functional communication training. *Journal of Applied Behavior Analysis, 18*, 111-26.

Newman B. and Reinecke, D. R. (2012). *Move with a purpose: Solving common behavior issues before they become unmanageable*. New York: Dove and Orca.

Newman, B. & Reinecke, D.R. (2007). *Behavioral detectives: A staff training exercise book in Applied Behavior Analysis*. New York: Dove and Orca.

Newman, B., Reeve, K. F., Reeve, S. A., & Ryan, C. S. (2003). *Behaviorspeak: A glossary of terms in Applied Behavior Analysis*. New York: Dove and Orca.

Newman, B., Reinecke, D. R., & Hammond, T. (2005). *Behaviorask: Straight answers to your ABA programming questions*. New York: Dove and Orca.

## About the Author

Dr. Bobby Newman is a Board Certified Behavior Analyst and Licensed Psychologist. Affectionately known as the Dark Overlord of ABA, Bobby is the first author on eleven books regarding behavior therapy, the philosophy of behaviorism, the autism spectrum disorders, and utopian literature. He has published over two dozen articles in professional journals, as well as numerous popular magazine articles and has hosted two series of radio call-in shows. Bobby is the Past-President of the Association for Science in Autism Treatment and the New York State Association for Behavior Analysis. A popular speaker, Bobby also provides direct treatment, staff training and consultation around the world, and has been honored for this work by several parents and professional groups. He is the director of Room to Grow. Bobby is also a certified personal trainer and marathoner and is an Ambassador for the Great Sportsmanship Programme. Bobby teaches non-violent crisis intervention philosophy and techniques for agencies and families.

Made in the USA
Lexington, KY
30 June 2014